M000049939

TO AN AMAZING TEACHER:

_____

_____

FROM:

_____

Published by Christian Art Publishers
PO Box 1599, Vereeniging, 1930, RSA

© 2020
First edition 2020

Designed by Christian Art Publishers
Cover designed by Christian Art Publishers
Images used under license from Shutterstock.com

Scripture quotations are taken from the *Holy Bible*, New Living
Translation, copyright © 1996, 2004, 2015 by Tyndale House
Foundation. Used by permission of Tyndale House Publishers,
Inc., Carol Stream, Illinois 60188. All rights reserved.

Scripture quotations are taken from the *Holy Bible*, New
International Version®, NIV® Copyright © 1973, 1978, 1984,
2011 by Biblica, Inc.® Used by permission. All rights reserved
worldwide.

Scripture quotations are taken from the *Holy Bible*,
English Standard Version®. ESV® Text Edition: 2016.
Copyright © 2001 by Crossway, a publishing ministry of Good
News Publishers. Used by permission. All rights reserved.

Printed in China

ISBN 978-1-4321-3156-2

20 21 22 23 24 25 26 27 28 29 – 10 9 8 7 6 5 4 3 2 1

Printed in Jiaxing, China
October 2019
Print Run: 100588

NOTES
to an

A+
Teacher

CHRISTIAN ART
PUBLISHERS

Thank you
for teaching me to:

A TEACHER
takes a hand,
opens a mind
and touches a

heart

Teachers

are a

bright light,

a friendly

FACE

& A GENTLE GUIDE.

Commit

to the **LORD**
whatever you do,
and He will
establish your plans.

PROVERBS 16:3

You deserve the

award

Work willingly at
WHATEVER YOU DO,
as though you were

working

for the
Lord
rather than for people.

Colossians 3:23

You can TEACH
a LESSON for a day,
but if you TEACH

curiosity,

you TEACH
for a

lifetime.

The mediocre teacher tells.
The good teacher explains.
The superior teacher demonstrates.

THE GREAT
TEACHER

inspires.

William Arthur Ward

You give the
best advice on:

_____

_____

_____

_____

_____

_____

_____

DELIGHT

YOURSELF

IN THE LORD,

and HE will give you
the desires of your

HEART.

PSALM 37:4

It's the
SUPREME ART
of the
teacher
to awaken joy in
CREATIVE EXPRESSION
& knowledge.

ALBERT EINSTEIN

TEACH.
NURTURE.
INSPIRE.
ENCOURAGE.
PRAISE.
MOTIVATE.

Trust
IN THE LORD
WITH ALL YOUR HEART;
do not depend on your
own understanding.
SEEK HIS WILL
IN ALL YOU DO
& HE WILL
show you which
PATH TO TAKE.

Proverbs 3:5-6

YOUR WORD IS A *lamp* TO GUIDE MY FEET AND A *light* FOR MY PATH.

Psalm 119:105

Thank you

for setting a
GOOD

example.

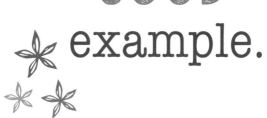

Encourage
each other
 **BUILD**
EACH OTHER UP,
just as you are
already doing.

1 Thessalonians 5:11

They
may forget
what you said,
but they will
never forget
how you made
them feel.

Carl Buehner

Be somebody

WHO MAKES

everybody

FEEL LIKE A

somebody

...

You are
the
best at:

_____

_____

_____

_____

In **His**
grace,
God has
GIVEN US
different **gifts**
FOR DOING CERTAIN THINGS WELL...
If you are a teacher,
TEACH WELL.
Romans 12:6-7

TELL ME AND
I FORGET.
TEACH ME
AND I REMEMBER.
Involve me
AND I LEARN.

BENJAMIN FRANKLIN

TEACHING
is a work
of
heart

TEACHERS WHO LOVE

teaching,
TEACH
CHILDREN TO LOVE
LEARNING.

I will always
remember how you ...

DIRECT

your children
onto the

RIGHT PATH,

and when they are older,
they will not leave it.

Proverbs 22:6

Success
is the sum of
SMALL EFFORTS,
REPEATED
day in and
day out.

ROBERT COLLIER

YOU

encourage
me to:

_____

_____

_____

_____

_____

WHAT WE LEARN BECOMES A PART OF WHO WE ARE.

Let the
message about
CHRIST,
in all its richness,
FILL YOUR LIVES.
TEACH
& counsel each
other with
ALL THE WISDOM
HE gives.
COLOSSIANS 3:16

KIND
WORDS
can be short
and easy to speak,
but their echoes
are truly endless.

MOTHER TERESA

BY DOING
WHAT YOU LOVE,
YOU INSPIRE
& AWAKEN THE
HEARTS OF
OTHERS.

TAKE
HOLD OF MY
INSTRUCTIONS;
DON'T LET THEM GO.
GUARD THEM,
FOR THEY ARE THE
KEY TO LIFE.

PROVERBS 4:13

BE
THE KIND OF
LEADER
YOU WOULD
WANT TO
FOLLOW.

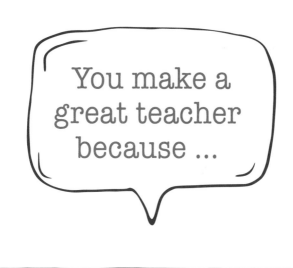

You make a
great teacher
because ...

_____

_____

_____

_____

_____

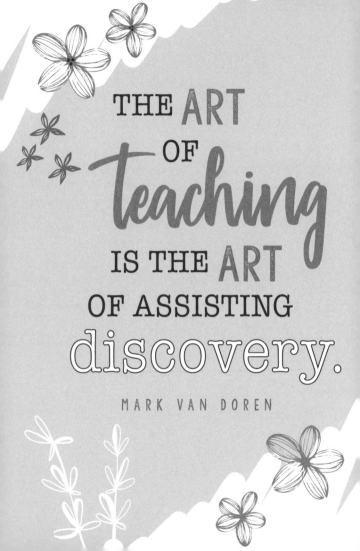

THE ART
OF
teaching
IS THE ART
OF ASSISTING
discovery.

MARK VAN DOREN

So commit yourselves

WHOLEHEARTEDLY

to these

words

OF MINE.

Tie them to your hands
and wear them on your forehead
as reminders.

Deuteronomy 11:18

In a
world where
YOU CAN BE
anything,
be
KIND.

Give
ALL YOUR
worries and cares
TO GOD,
FOR HE CARES
about you.

1 PETER 5:7

YOU MAKE

learning

FUN

"DON'T BE AFRAID,
FOR I AM WITH YOU.
DON'T BE DISCOURAGED,
FOR I AM YOUR GOD.
I WILL STRENGTHEN YOU
AND HELP YOU.
I WILL HOLD YOU UP WITH MY
VICTORIOUS RIGHT HAND."

ISAIAH 41:10

Together
MAY WE GIVE
OUR children
THE ROOTS
TO grow
AND THE WINGS
TO fly.

IF YOUR ACTIONS
INSPIRE CHILDREN
TO DREAM MORE,
LEARN MORE,
DO MORE AND
BECOME MORE,
YOU ARE INDEED
WORTHY OF THE
TITLE OF "TEACHER."

I CAN DO
everything
through CHRIST
who gives me
STRENGTH.

PHILIPPIANS 4:13

IT TAKES
A BIG
heart
to help shape
little minds.

I think
you are really
amazing.

"**COME TO ME,**
all of you who are
weary and carry
heavy burdens,
AND I WILL
GIVE
you rest."

MATTHEW 11:28

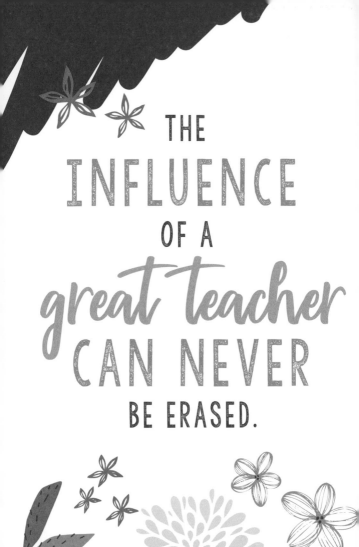

THE
INFLUENCE
OF A
great teacher
CAN NEVER
BE ERASED.

THE WHOLE PURPOSE OF

EDUCATION

IS TO TURN

mirrors

INTO

WINDOWS.

SYDNEY J. HARRIS

Thank you
for being such an
IMPORTANT
part of my
story.

For God
has not given us
a spirit of fear
and timidity, but of

POWER,
LOVE,
and self-discipline.

2 TIMOTHY 1:7

Teacher,

I will always remember you for ...

_____

_____

_____

_____

_____

_____

THE LORD HIMSELF WILL FIGHT FOR YOU. JUST STAY CALM.

EXODUS 14:14

TEACHERS

help students find

IMPORTANT
THINGS

they've lost every day.
Sometimes it's a paper,
backpack or jacket.

**OTHER TIMES IT IS
COURAGE, CONFIDENCE
OR A SMILE.**

A TEACHER
affects eternity;
HE CAN NEVER
tell where his
INFLUENCE
stops.

HENRY ADAMS

"I AM
WITH YOU

always,

EVEN TO THE
END OF THE AGE."

Matthew 28:20

No matter what,
you always know how
to make me feel ...

GOOD

teachers

know how to bring out the

BEST

IN STUDENTS.

The true aim of
EVERYONE WHO
aspires
to be a
TEACHER
SHOULD BE,
not to impart his own
opinions, but to

kindle minds.

FREDERICK W. ROBERTSON

Teacher,

you cheer me up
and encourage me when ...

_____

_____

_____

_____

_____

SO, MY DEAR
BROTHERS AND SISTERS,
BE STRONG AND IMMOVABLE.
ALWAYS WORK ENTHUSIASTICALLY
FOR THE LORD, FOR YOU KNOW
THAT NOTHING YOU DO FOR THE
LORD IS EVER USELESS.

1 CORINTHIANS 15:58

For the LORD YOUR GOD is living among you. HE IS A MIGHTY SAVIOR. He will *rejoice* over you with joyful songs.

ZEPHANIAH 3:17

TIME SPENT with *children* IS NEVER wasted.

LOVE

IS A

GREAT

TEACHER

ST. AUGUSTINE

Teachers
are
PRECIOUS PEOPLE
who cause
JOYFUL
HAPPENINGS
in the hearts of
children.

You are a
GREAT
encourager.

This is the

DAY

THE LORD

HAS MADE.

We will

rejoice

and be

glad in it.

PSALM 118:24

LOVE

ALWAYS PROTECTS,
ALWAYS TRUSTS,
ALWAYS HOPES,
ALWAYS PERSEVERES.

I CORINTHIANS 13:7

THE LORD GIVES
STRENGTH
TO HIS PEOPLE;
THE LORD
BLESSES
HIS PEOPLE WITH
PEACE.

PSALM 29:11

Great works
are performed
not by strength,
but by
PERSEVERANCE.

SAMUEL JOHNSON

"**Give,**
and it will be
GIVEN
to you.
For with the
measure you use
it will be measured
back to you."

LUKE 6:38

My favorite day in your class was when ...

_____

_____

_____

_____

_____

_____

_____

_____

The faithful love of the LORD never ends! His mercies never cease. Great is His faithfulness; His mercies begin afresh each morning.

LAMENTATIONS 3:22-23

Every tomorrow
has two handles.
We can take hold
of it by the handle
of anxiety, or by
the handle of

faith.

HENRY WARD BEECHER

FIX YOUR

thoughts

on what is true, and honorable,
and right, and pure,
and lovely, and admirable.

Think

about things that are excellent
and worthy of praise.

PHILIPPIANS 4:8

"For I know the
PLANS I have for you,"
declares the **LORD**,
"PLANS to *prosper* you
and not to harm you,
PLANS to give you *hope*
and a *future."*

JEREMIAH 29:11

I THANK GOD
for you
& *pray*
THAT HE WILL
always
BLESS YOU!

"BE STRONG
AND COURAGEOUS.
DO NOT BE AFRAID;
DO NOT BE DISCOURAGED,
FOR THE LORD YOUR GOD
WILL BE WITH YOU
WHEREVER YOU GO."

JOSHUA 1:9

FEAR
OF THE LORD
is the
FOUNDATION
OF TRUE
knowledge.

PROVERBS 1:7

Because of you,
I've learned ...

_____

_____

_____

_____

_____

_____

INSTRUCT THE WISE
AND THEY WILL BE WISER STILL:
TEACH THE RIGHTEOUS
AND THEY WILL ADD
TO THEIR LEARNING.

PROVERBS 9:9

The best teachers

ARE THOSE WHO

show you

WHERE TO LOOK,
BUT DON'T TELL YOU

what to see.

"LET YOUR
light shine
BEFORE OTHERS,
THAT THEY MAY SEE YOUR
GOOD DEEDS
and glorify
YOUR FATHER IN HEAVEN."

MATTHEW 5:16

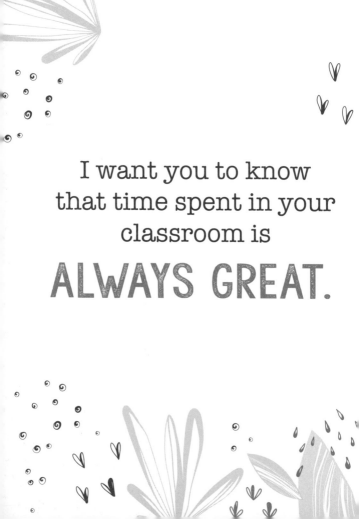

I want you to know
that time spent in your
classroom is

ALWAYS GREAT.

"Be still,
and know
that
I AM GOD!"

PSALM 46:10

Worry weighs
a person down;
an encouraging
word cheers
a person up.

Proverbs 12:25

Blessed

are those who
TRUST IN THE LORD
and have made the

LORD

THEIR HOPE
AND CONFIDENCE.

Jeremiah 17:7

The best life lesson
I've learned from you was ...

_____

_____

_____

_____

_____

_____

STRIVE FOR

progress

not perfection.

WHEN I GROW UP
I WANT TO BE AS ...

_____

_____

AS YOU.

IT'S NOT HOW MUCH YOU DO,
but how much

love

YOU PUT INTO THE

doing
that matters.

MOTHER TERESA

The **BEST**
teachers
TEACH
from the heart,
not from the book.